PLANETS

SATURN

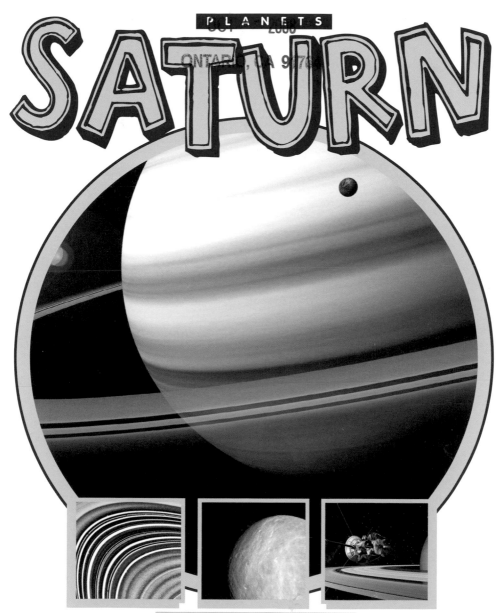

ABDO
Publishing Company

A Buddy Book by Fran Howard

VISIT US AT

www.abdopublishing.com

Published by ABDO Publishing Company, 8000 West 78th Street, Edina, Minnesota 55439.

Printed in the United States.

Editor: Sarah Tieck
Contributing Editor: Michael P. Goecke
Graphic Design: Maria Hosley
Cover Image: Photodisc.
Interior Images: NASA: Headquarters—Greatest Images Of NASA (page 9, 25), Jet Propulsion Laboratory (page 6–7, 12, 17, 27, 28, 30), JPL / Space Science Institute (page 11, 12, 13, 16, 17), Marshall Space Flight Center (page 5, 25, 29); Library of Congress (page 23); Lushpix (page 11).

Library of Congress Cataloging-in-Publication Data

Howard, Fran, 1953-
  Saturn / Fran Howard.
     p. cm. -- (The planets)
  Includes index.
  ISBN 978-1-59928-828-4
  1. Saturn (Planet)--Juvenile literature. I. Title.

  QB671.H69 2008
  523.46--dc22

                                        2007014759

Table Of Contents

The Planet Saturn

Saturn is a planet. A planet is a large body in space.

Planets travel around stars. The path a planet travels is its orbit. When the planet circles a star, it is orbiting the star.

The sun is a star. Saturn orbits the sun. The sun's **gravity** holds Saturn in place as it circles.

Saturn takes about 29.5 Earth years to orbit the sun. That means a year on Saturn is about thirty times as long as a year on Earth!

The atmosphere on Saturn has some sulfur in it. This makes the planet appear yellow.

Our Solar System

OUTER PLANETS

Neptune
Uranus
Saturn
Jupiter

Saturn's Orbit

Saturn is one of eight planets that orbit our sun. The planets orbiting the sun make up our solar system.

The other planets in our solar system are Mercury, Venus, Earth, Mars, Jupiter, Uranus, and Neptune.

Saturn is about 888 million miles (1,400,000,000 km) from the sun. It is the sixth-closest planet to the sun.

SUN

Mars

Earth

Venus

Mercury

INNER PLANETS

Thousands Of Rings

Saturn has seven main ring groups. These are made up of thousands of "ringlets." The seven main rings are separated by gaps.

Saturn's rings are made mostly of rocks and ice. Some of the rocks and ice are the size of dust. Other pieces are as big as cars!

Saturn's rings extend out thousands of miles from the planet. But, they are less than one mile (2 km) thick. The ice in the rings reflects the sun's light in interesting ways. This makes Saturn's rings very colorful.

Scientists think Saturn's rings might have formed when a moon exploded.

A Closer Look

Saturn is the second-largest planet in the solar system. Jupiter is the largest.

Saturn spins rapidly on its **axis**. This spinning flattens the planet at the top and bottom. It also makes Saturn bulge near the middle.

Sometimes, huge storms happen on Saturn. These storms cover areas as large as Earth! They are called Great White Spots. Scientists think these storms happen about every 30 years.

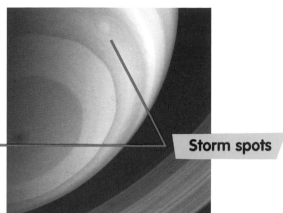

Storm spots

Saturn has the fastest winds in our solar system. They are five times faster than hurricane winds on Earth.

Saturn has many moons. Scientists aren't sure exactly how many. But, they have identified 47 moons for sure.

Many of Saturn's moons are very small. Some of them are more like huge rocks.

Rhea orbits Saturn.

Enceladus *(left)*, Rhea *(center)*, and Tethys *(right)* are three of Saturn's known moons.

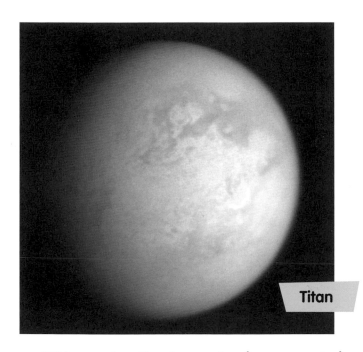

Titan

Titan is Saturn's largest-known moon. It is about as wide as the United States. That means it is larger than the planet Mercury!

Titan is the second-largest moon in the solar system. Ganymede, one of Jupiter's moons, is the largest.

What Is It Like There?

Layers of gases surround each planet. These layers form the planet's **atmosphere**. The atmosphere on Saturn has multiple bands of gases.

A planet spins on an **axis**. This spinning creates night and day.

Saturn takes about 10 hours and 47 minutes to make a complete spin. That is less than half the length of a day on Earth.

Saturn takes about 11 Earth hours to make one rotation on its axis.

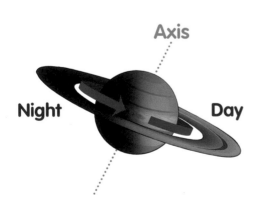

Axis

Night

Day

THE SUN

Saturn makes more heat than it gets from the sun. Saturn's south pole is the hottest place on the planet. A strange hot spot covers this pole. This hot spot is the first to be discovered in our solar system. Scientists are not sure what causes it.

Earth's poles are colder than the rest of the planet. For some reason, Saturn's south pole is hotter than the rest of the planet.

Scientists think seasonal changes cause the color differences between Saturn's top and bottom halves.

A Gas Giant

Scientists think Saturn may have a rocky core. But, it does not have a surface to stand on.

This is because Saturn is a gas giant. Gas giants are mostly made of gas. Jupiter, Uranus, and Neptune are also gas giants.

The center of Saturn is very hot. Its temperature can reach 21,092 degrees Fahrenheit (11,700°C)! Above the center is a liquid layer, followed by the gas layer. Above this, the **atmosphere** forms the outer layer.

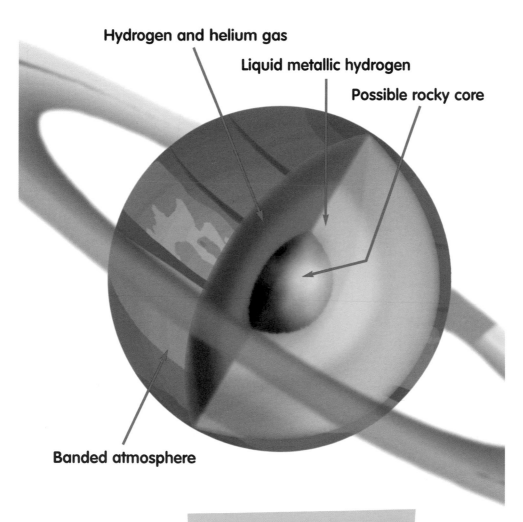

Hydrogen and helium gas

Liquid metallic hydrogen

Possible rocky core

Banded atmosphere

Gas giants have layers, but
no surfaces to stand on.

Discovering Saturn

No one knows who discovered Saturn. But, it is visible in Earth's night sky. So, people on Earth have known about it since early times.

The Romans named Saturn after their god of farming.

On a clear night, it is possible to see Saturn without using a telescope.

In 1659, Christiaan Huygens thought Saturn had one big ring circling it.

In 1675, Jean-Dominique Cassini discovered that Saturn's ring was actually many small rings.

Almost 200 years later, James Clerk Maxwell also studied Saturn's rings. He determined that they are made of small objects.

Galileo was the first person to see Saturn's rings.
He saw them through a telescope in 1610.

Missions To Saturn

In 1979, *Pioneer 11* became the first **spacecraft** to fly by Saturn. It studied Saturn's rings. It also measured the temperature of the moon Titan.

In 1980, *Voyager 1* took images of Saturn, its rings, and its moons. *Voyager 1* also flew close to Titan. It discovered that clouds cover this moon.

One year later, *Voyager 2* took more images of Saturn and its rings.

Voyager 2 launched in 1977.

Voyager 2 photographed the four outer planets during a flyby.

Scientists have learned a lot about Saturn, its rings, and its moons from the *Cassini-Huygens* **mission**. The mission's **spacecraft** launched in 1997. In 2004, it reached Saturn.

The *Cassini-Huygens* spacecraft sent a **probe** to Titan on December 25, 2004. The probe found liquid **methane** and evidence of **precipitation**. It also discovered that some of Titan's rocks are actually made of frozen water.

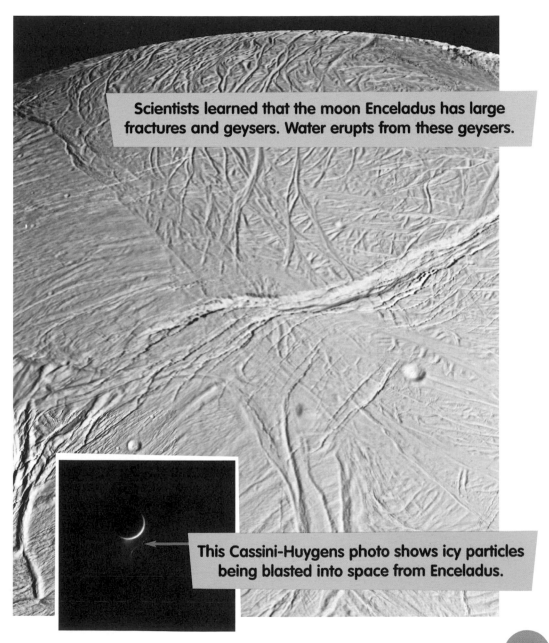

Scientists learned that the moon Enceladus has large fractures and geysers. Water erupts from these geysers.

This Cassini-Huygens photo shows icy particles being blasted into space from Enceladus.

Fact Trek

The symbol for Saturn is a sickle. Long ago, farmers used sickles to harvest grain.

With a good pair of binoculars or a small telescope, you can see Saturn's rings from Earth.

Saturn is a very light planet. If it were placed in water, Saturn would float.

Every 14 years, Saturn's rings seem to disappear. This happens when the rings face Earth edge on.

Saturn's major rings are only 330 feet (100 m) thick.

Voyage To Tomorrow

People are continuing to explore space. They want to learn more about Saturn.

The *Cassini-Huygens* **spacecraft** began orbiting Saturn on July 1, 2004. By the end of its **mission** in 2008, it orbited Saturn 74 times.

The Cassini-Huygens spacecraft flew by Venus, Earth, and Jupiter before reaching Saturn.

Important Words

atmosphere   the layer of gases that surrounds a planet.

axis   an imaginary line through a planet. Planets spin around this line.

gravity   the force that draws things toward a planet and prevents them from floating away. Stars use this force to keep planets in their orbit.

methane   an odorless, colorless gas that burns easily. Sometimes it is used for fuel.

mission   the sending of spacecraft to perform specific jobs.

precipitation   rain, snow, or other moisture that falls from the sky.

probe   a spacecraft that attempts to gather information.

spacecraft   a vehicle that travels in space.

Web Sites

To learn more about **Saturn**, visit ABDO Publishing Company on the World Wide Web. Web sites about **Saturn** are featured on our Book Links page. These links are routinely monitored and updated to provide the most current information available.

www.abdopublishing.com

INDEX